A Bug's World

Spin with the Spiders

By Karen Latchana Kenney
Illustrated by Lisa Hedicker

Content Consultant
Clyde Sorenson, PhD
Professor of Entomology
North Carolina State University

magic wagon

visit us at www.abdopublishing.com

Published by Magic Wagon, a division of the ABDO Group, 8000 West 78th Street, Edina, Minnesota 55439.
Copyright © 2011 by Abdo Consulting Group, Inc. International copyrights reserved in all countries. All rights
reserved. No part of this book may be reproduced in any form without written permission from the publisher.

Looking Glass Library™ is a trademark and logo of Magic Wagon.

Printed in the United States of America, North Mankato, Minnesota.
042010
092010

Text by Karen Latchana Kenney
Illustrations by Lisa Hedicker
Edited by Amy Van Zee
Interior layout and design by Becky Daum
Cover design by Becky Daum

Library of Congress Cataloging-in-Publication Data
Kenney, Karen Latchana.
 Spin with the spiders / by Karen Latchana Kenney ; illustrated by Lisa Hedicker.
    p. cm. — (A bug's world)
 Includes index.
 ISBN 978-1-60270-789-4
 1. Spiders—Juvenile literature. I. Hedicker, Lisa, 1984– , ill. II. Title.
 QL458.4.K46 2011
 595.4'4—dc22
                        2009052918

Table of Contents

Creeping and Crawling

Spiders crawl around deserts, caves, and forests. They live inside houses, too. Spiders come in all sizes and colors. There are more than 35,000 kinds of spiders on Earth. Some live for much less than a year. Others can live for more than 20 years.

A spider is not an insect like an ant or a bee. Insects have six legs, but spiders have eight. An insect's body has three main sections. A spider's has two. But, spiders and insects are all arthropods.

5

Growing Spiders

A silky, white egg sac hangs high in a tree. Inside, hundreds of spiderlings are hatching from their eggs. They stay inside the egg sac while they grow and change. To grow, a spiderling's skin breaks open. The spiderling crawls out. The new skin will soon grow hard.

The spiderlings are ready to leave the egg sac. They use their fangs to cut open the silky, white threads and crawl out.

Spiders molt again after they leave
the egg sac. They molt several
times as they become adults.

The spiderlings are hungry. But there are not enough bugs nearby for all of them to eat. Some of them must go away to find prey.

These spiderlings spin long lines of silk. The wind catches the silk, and the baby spiders are lifted high into the air. In this way, they travel fast and far.

Web Builders

Spin, spin, spin. Some spiders build webs to trap their prey.

To build a web, a spider shoots silk out of its spinnerets. These parts look like little fingers at the back end of the spider. The silk starts as a liquid. Then it becomes a strong, hard thread.

Many spiders build round webs called orb webs. Some of the threads are sticky, and some are dry. A bug flies into the web. The sticky threads trap the insect so it cannot fly away. Then the spider walks on the dry threads to reach its prey. It wraps the insect in silk to keep it from moving.

A spider makes different kinds of silk.
Swathing silk is used to wrap food.
Another type keeps eggs safe.

Hunters

Some spiders hunt for food instead of catching it in webs. Some hunters use their eyes to help them find prey. Most spiders have eight eyes. Other spiders have six, four, or two eyes. Some of the eyes sense movement. Other eyes let the spider know how far away the prey is.

eyes

Spiders also use tiny hairs on their legs to sense the world around them. A spider uses these hairs to touch, like fingers. The hairs can smell, too.

A spider hides and waits to feel the air move or a leaf shake. It knows that bugs are moving around. Then the spider jumps out and catches its prey.

hairs on legs

A fishing spider is walking on water! This strong spider may dive underwater to grab tadpoles and small fish.

A jumping spider leaps to catch its food. It can jump more than 40 times the length of its body.

Another type of spider spits sticky venom to trap its prey. The venom makes its prey stop moving.

A spider has caught a bug. The spider holds its food with its palps and jaws. Each jaw has a sharp fang. The spider shoots venom through the fangs into its prey.

The bug goes still. Its insides become liquid. A spider does not have teeth, so it drinks up its meal.

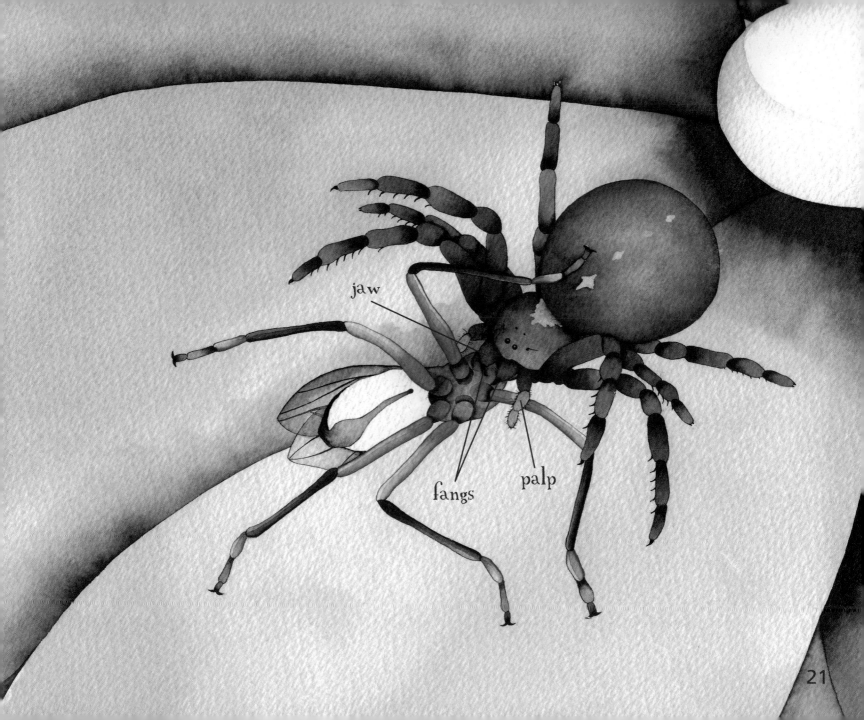

jaw

fangs

palp

Staying Safe

Spiders are hunters, but they are also food for larger creatures. Their predators include birds, lizards, other spiders, and many other animals.

Spiders have special ways of fooling predators. Some spiders walk on six legs to look like an ant. Some look like bird droppings.

Spiders can blend in with the things
around them. They may be out in the
open, but predators cannot see them.

23

Spiders can also use their silk to stay safe. A spider in a web spins a thread of silk behind it. This is called a dragline. When danger is near, the spider drops on the dragline. When the danger is gone, the spider climbs back up to its web.

Some spiders build a web to help protect their egg sacs. This is called a nursery web.

New Lives

A female spider's life is nearing its end. She finds a safe spot to lay her eggs. The mother wraps the group of eggs in strong silk to protect them. Then the spider attaches the egg sacs to a branch. She might die before the eggs hatch.

Inside the egg sacs, the spiderlings will grow, hatch, and molt. They will crawl out of their egg sacs and begin their lives.

A Spider's Body

There are two parts of a spider's body. The front is called the cephalothorax. The back part is the abdomen. The spider's body is covered in a hard, protective casing. It is tough, like fingernails.

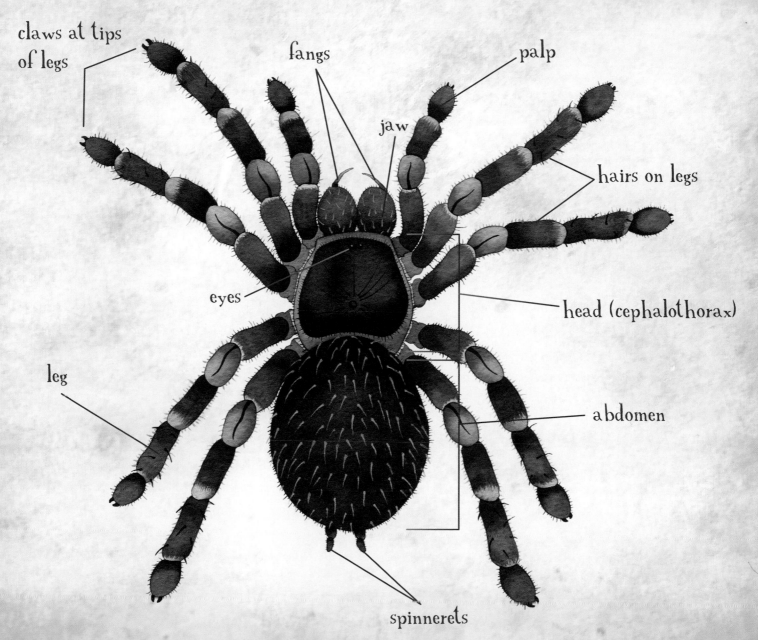

claws at tips of legs

fangs

palp

jaw

hairs on legs

eyes

head (cephalothorax)

leg

abdomen

spinnerets

29

A Closer Look

Comparing Arachnids

What you will need:

- picture of a spider
- picture of a scorpion
- notebook paper
- pencil

Spiders and scorpions are arachnids. They have two body parts and eight legs. Parts of their bodies are alike. Other parts are different. Let's compare the two!

Draw a line down the middle of a piece of paper. Title one side "Alike" and the other side "Different." Look at the pictures of the spider and the scorpion. Be sure to look at these body parts:

- legs
- head
- abdomen
- eyes
- palps

Write the things that look the same on the "Alike" side of the paper. Write the things that do not look the same on the "Different" side of the paper. See what else you can find!

Spider Facts

- The Goliath bird-eating spider is one of the biggest spiders. It can be 10 inches (25 cm) across. It lives in South America. This spider is so big, it can eat small birds.
- The Samoan moss spider is one of the smallest spiders. It is 0.1 inch (0.3 cm) wide. That is about the size of a pinhead.

Glossary

abdomen—the back part of an arthropod's body.

fang—a long, sharp tooth.

molt—to break out of a layer of skin so that new, bigger skin can grow.

palps—leg-like body parts that a spider uses to hold things.

spiderling—a young spider.

spinneret—either of the two body parts attached to the abdomen of a spider where the silk is made.

venom—a poison produced by some animals and insects. It usually enters a victim through a bite or sting.

On the Web

To learn more about spiders, visit ABDO Group online at **www.abdopublishing.com**. Web sites about spiders are featured on our Book Links page. These links are routinely monitored and updated to provide the most current information available.

Index